MYTHS UNDERSTOOD

UNDERSTANDING NATIVE AMERICAN MYTHS

MEGAN KOPP

Crabtree Publishing Company

www.crabtreebooks.com

Author: Megan Kopp
Publishing plan research and development:
    Sean Charlebois, Reagan Miller
    Crabtree Publishing Company
Editor-in-chief: Lionel Bender
Editors: Simon Adams, Lynn Peppas
Proofreaders: Laura Booth, Wendy Scavuzzo
Project coordinator: Kathy Middleton
Photo research: Kim Richardson
Designer: Ben White
Cover design: Margaret Amy Salter
Production coordinator and Prepress technician:
    Samara Parent
Production: Kim Richardson
Print coordinator: Katherine Berti

Consultants: Amy Leggett-Caldera, M.Ed., Elementary
and Middle School Education Consultant, Mississippi
State University.

Cover: Bald Eagle (top middle); Bison (bottom left);
Totem Pole (bottom middle); Coyote (bottom right);
Native North American tipis (middle center)

Title page: Haida Totem Pole

Photographs and reproductions:
Cover: Thinkstock (except middle center); Shutterstock (middle center)
Maps: Stefan Chabluk
Getty Images: 11
Library of Congress: 23 (LC-USZ62-50348), 24b (LC-USZ62-88073), 42b
(LC-USZC4-8937).
shutterstock.com: 1 (Leene), 4 (CreativeHQ), 6t (karamysh), 10t (Dennis
Tokarzewski), 16 (Rago Arts), 21 (Jamen Percy), 24t (Rago Arts), 30
(Duncan Gilbert), 36t (John C. Hooten), 36b (Josemaria Toscano), 40t
(Ryan Richter), 40b (RIRF Stock), 41 (Katrina Brown), 42t (Lori Martin).
Topfoto (Fortean/Aarsleff): 31; (The Granger Collection): 5l, 8, 13, 26,
27, 28, 32, 34, 35, 38, 39; (Imageworks): 5r, 10b, 17; (topfoto.co.uk): 6b;
10, 44 r, (ullsteinbild): 33.
Werner Forman Archive: 13 (Centennial Museum, Vancouver, British
Columbia, Canada), 14 (Maxwell Museum of Anthropology,
Albuquerque), 17 (Arizona State Museum), 18 (Provincial Museum,
Victoria, British Columbia, Canada), 20 (Sheldon Jackson Museum,
Sitka, Alaska), 22 (Field Museum of Natural History, Chicago), 29
(Field Museum of Natural History, Chicago), 37 (Museum of the
American Indian, Heye Foundation, New York), 44 (Private
Collection).

This book was produced for Crabtree Publishing Company
by Bender Richardson White

Library and Archives Canada Cataloguing in Publication

Kopp, Megan
    Understanding native American myths / Megan Kopp.

(Myths understood)
Includes index.
Issued also in electronic formats.
ISBN 978-0-7787-4526-6 (bound).--ISBN 978-0-7787-4531-0 (pbk.)

    1. Indian mythology--North America--Juvenile literature.
2. Indians of North America--Religion--Juvenile literature.
I. Title. II. Series: Myths understood

E98.R3K66 2012   j299.7   C2012-906375-4

Library of Congress Cataloging-in-Publication Data

CIP available at Library of Congress

Crabtree Publishing Company

www.crabtreebooks.com   1-800-387-7650

Printed in the U.S.A./112012/FA20121012

Published in Canada
Crabtree Publishing
616 Welland Ave.
St. Catharines, Ontario
L2M 5V6

Published in the United States
Crabtree Publishing
PMB 59051
350 Fifth Avenue, 59th Floor
New York, New York 10118

Published in the United Kingdom
Crabtree Publishing
Maritime House
Basin Road North, Hove
BN41 1WR

Published in Australia
Crabtree Publishing
3 Charles Street
Coburg North
VIC 3058

CONTENTS

WHAT ARE MYTHS?

Myths are ancient stories passed down through many generations. Most are so old that they began as spoken tales. Myths are stories that help people make sense of their lives.

Without myths, ancient people would have been bothered by unknowns. Topics such as the creation of Earth, the Sun, and the stars, the origins of humankind, and life and death, would have been very difficult for them to understand. Myths also shaped their beliefs and traditions.

There were several thousand different **tribes** of people living in North America prior to European contact in the 1500s C.E. Each tribe had its own **mythology**.

Native American myths are rooted in nature and the belief that everything— living or nonliving—has a **spirit**. Many Native American **ceremonies** were based on myths. Native American mythology, **ritual**, ceremonies, and **religion** are often difficult to separate. Navajo ceremonies, such as Blessingway, which is concerned with healing, creation, and peace, are based on events and incidents in their mythology.

NAMING THE PEOPLE

Native Americans were referred to as Indians or American Indians in the United States for centuries after Italian explorer Christopher Columbus mistakenly thought he had arrived in the Indies in 1492. He referred to the people he saw as *los indios*. In Canada, aboriginal or early native people as a group are referred to as First Nations.

Many Native American myths are related to the belief that all animals have **souls** or spirits that give them supernatural powers. Myths about gods who control the elements are also common. The close connection animals and the weather had in people's daily lives influenced their survival, which is why these topics figure so prominently in Native American mythologies.

Other countries have mythologies shaped and ordered by traditional authors over many centuries. In North America, few myths were written down before the late 1800s. The myths still reflect strong roots in the oral tradition of storytelling.

Stories told on long winter's nights around campfires taught about right from wrong and helped explain why things happened the way they did. The myths also helped keep ancient beliefs alive, and they entertained. Native American storytelling involved a range of accompaniments, including dance, masks, costumes, and music. Humor was also used.

Below: On a Pribilof island near Alaska, a traditional Aleut storyteller and environmental **activist** uses a drum to tell his mythological tale to young people.

Left: A photograph from 1906 shows an Apache elder marking the ground with a stick while explaining to fellow tribesmen an ancient myth about the landscape.

According to archaeologists**, the first people of North America arrived in the far northwest about 20,000 to 60,000 years ago. Now called Paleo-Indians, they crossed the Bering Strait land bridge from Asia. Small, scattered communities slowly became established across great distances and in vastly different environments.**

It is believed the Inuit (formerly called Eskimo), Aleut, and Athabascan peoples migrated to Arctic North America by boat, arriving around 10,000 years ago. These hunters relied on marine mammals, caribou, birds, and fish for their survival. Later, Subarctic cultures formed, including the western Athabascan-speaking tribes and the eastern Algonquin-speaking people. Using snowshoes and canoes, they hunted moose, deer, and fish.

Tribes of the Pacific Northwest lived in an area of mild climate with cool summers and wet winters. These tribes were hunter-gatherers, harvesting food from the land and sea. Inland, tribes of the Great Basin and Plateau lived in harsher, semidesert conditions. They survived on fish, small game, nuts, and seeds.

TRAVEL BEFORE HORSES

Dogs were an important part of early Native American tribal life. Before horses, Plains tribes used dogs to haul their **travois**, or sled, carrying food and belongings. In the Pacific Northwest, the Tahltan bear dog was a scrappy little fighter used for tracking and hunting bears. The Qimmiq or Inuit dog hauled sleds for Arctic tribes. Why Dogs do Not Speak is a Kiowa myth, one of many dog tales in Native American mythology.

Below: A Cree native North American mother with her children and dogs stands outside the family tepee. This photograph was taken in the early 1900s.

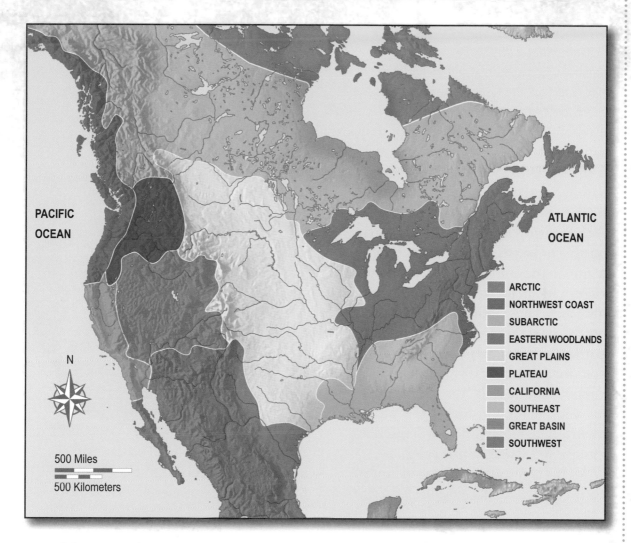

PACIFIC
OCEAN

ATLANTIC
OCEAN

N

500 Miles

500 Kilometers

- ARCTIC
- NORTHWEST COAST
- SUBARCTIC
- EASTERN WOODLANDS
- GREAT PLAINS
- PLATEAU
- CALIFORNIA
- SOUTHEAST
- GREAT BASIN
- SOUTHWEST

Californian tribes enjoyed a pleasant climate, with warm winters and abundant resources from the land and ocean. They did not need to travel far to find food.

In the Southwest, desert conditions brought long periods of drought and intense floods. Native American tribes hunted and tended crops of beans, squash, and corn. Across the Great Plains, many tribes were nomadic, always on the move following herds of bison, which they hunted for food, leather, and dung for fires.

Above: This map of North America shows the main geographical regions. Native peoples and tribes are usually referred to by region.

In the Northeast, summers were hot and winters cool. Tribes hunted deer and harvested corn and wild rice. To the Southeast, Native Americans such as the Seminole and Creek enjoyed good rainfall, hot, humid weather year-round, and abundant plant and animal life.

IN HARMONY WITH NATURE

Native Americans were aware of their natural surroundings, whether in the Arctic or on the Great Plains. As a result, there are common themes in their mythologies. The themes tell why things are the way they are in nature and include animals, plants, geographical features, the weather, and the Sun, Moon, and stars.

The myth could be about a natural cycle such as the cycle of light and dark in the north. During the darkest months of winter in the far north, the Sun never shines, and in the height of summer, it never sets. In an Inuit myth, Crow travels north and south. He knows about sunlight but, living in darkness, the northern people do not believe him. Crow steals a ball of light from the south. The ball drops releasing all the sunshine. Crow warns them it will not last and it will take six months to rebuild its power again.

Myths could also explain landforms such as Niagara Falls. One Iroquois myth

Above: A carved and painted wooden mask of the Kwakiutl tribe of British Columbia, Canada. The mask represents a sea monster.

suggests the falls were created after a struggle between the Thunder god and the Great Snake Monster. The thrashing of Snake Monster's tail scooped out the basin where the water falls. A myth could answer a question about a physical characteristic, for example the Choctaw myth about the theft of fire tells how smoke from the fire turned the crow's white feathers black.

BEYOND NATURE

Another common theme in Native American myths is the power associated

CREATION MYTHS

An enduring topic of all mythologies is the creation of the world. The Cherokee believed that a water-covered world was already in existence and soil was brought up from the depths by a water beetle to create the land. The Pueblo tribe believed that humans emerge into the present world from the **underworld**. The Siksika people believed in the creator god Napi, or Old Man.

THE HUNTER AND THE CHILDREN

Seals were a main source of food for early Inuit people living in the Arctic. This Inuit morality myth includes themes of respect, caring, and retribution.

The old hunter stood silently above the seal hole, harpoon raised and ready to strike. In the distance, children shouted with laughter. It distracted the hunter just as the seal surfaced. Glaring at the children playing below a snow-covered cliff, the hunter muttered, "I hope the snow falls off that cliff and buries those kids."

Nothing happened. The hunter resumed his watchful position above the seal's breathing hole. Again the seal returned, but the hunter was too busy thinking about the noisy play of the children. The seal saw the hunter and dove before the old man could react. Furious, the older hunter called upon the spirits that bring bad luck. "Bury those children under the snow." And it happened. An avalanche fell from the cliff and there was silence.

The parents of the children came running and when they realized what had happened they set out to find the old hunter. The hunter tried to flee but it was clear he could not escape. He called on his powers once more to lift him to the sky. The parents watched the old hunter rise in the sky, disappear briefly, and then reappear as a shooting star. On a clear night, you can still see the old hunter fleeing across the heavens.

with the Four Directions—North, South, East, and West. These are often represented by colors in many stories.

Cultural heroes are central to many myths. They often have supernatural powers, and they bring food or fire, teach skills, or kill monsters. For example, White Buffalo Woman is a cultural hero in Plains Indian mythology. She changed from a woman dressed in white buckskin into a white buffalo calf before the great herds of bison appeared.

Right: An Inuit man prepares his seal-skin kayak on Nunivak Island, Alaska.

RELIGION
AND
GODS

The everyday life of Native Americans involved a mixture of religion, customs, traditions, and beliefs. Sacred powers were found in everything, including the Sun and Moon, mountains, rivers, plants, and animals. Knowledge about the importance and diversity of spirits in the natural world was passed on in myths.

The Four Directions provide balance: East gave light, South warmth, West rain, and North gave strength, cold, and wind. The numbers four and seven are sacred for many Native Americans and are reflected in their myths. For example, Sweet Medicine spent four years away from his tribe. During that time, he gained much wisdom that he used to help his people.

Left: An Aleut elder leads boy and girl drummers during a celebration at the end of seal harvest, which collects meat for the community.

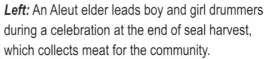

DRUMS AND DRUMMING

Drums are a part of many Native American ceremonies such as the Sun Dance for the Plains tribes (see page 35), Kachina dances among the Pueblo (page 28), and **shaman** rituals and **potlatch** feasts for Northwest Coast tribes. The Cherokee people have a myth called "The Daughter of the Sun" in which the Sun's daughter dies. Sun becomes sad and dark, but the sound of a drum brings a smile to her face and she shines again.

VISION QUEST

This Anishinabe myth from the Algonquin First Nation people highlights beliefs in sacred powers, cycles of life, and close connection between humans and animals.

Opichi's father was anxious for his son to receive the power from a vision. Before the last snow had left the ground, he sent Opichi off to build a shelter in the woods and wait for an animal spirit to take pity and offer guidance. That night, the North wind blew. When morning came, the father went to his son.

"I had a vision of a deer and it spoke to me," Opichi told his father.

"Good, but wait longer. There must be a greater vision."

Opichi stayed and that night snow fell. Again, in the morning, Opichi's father arrived and asked his son what he had seen. This time it was a beaver.

"Well done, but you will gain more power if you stay longer." Each morning the boy recited what he had seen. He grew thinner and weaker. Yet, every time, his father requested he stay a little longer in hopes of a greater vision.

On the final morning, Opichi's father walked through the woods to his son. Arriving at the shelter, he called out. There was no answer. He bent down to the door and a red-breasted bird flew out. It sang a new call that sounded much like his son's name, "Opi chi chi."

"My father, this is me now. The one who was your son is gone. You asked him to go too early and to wait too long. I will now return each spring to let parents know that it is time for their sons to go on their quest. It is your job to tell other parents not to let their sons stay out too long."

Time is circular, as is all life, in Native American culture. The seasons change in a circle. The Sun and Moon move in a circle. People are born, experience life, die, and the next generation repeats the cycle. Everything is connected in a circle.

Native Americans have many **rites of passage**, festivals, and ceremonies to mark important events, celebrate successes, and ensure good fortune. Navajo ceremonies such as Enemyway helped restore harmony and protect warriors.

A MULTITUDE OF GODS

Many myths are not about gods but about common people, events, and objects—all of which are gifted with a spirit. However, there are specific gods mentioned in Native American mythology.

The Lakota believed in Wakan Tanka, or The Great Mystery. In mythology, Wakan Tanka represented all spiritual beings and powers and was the Creator, or Great Spirit. The power or sacredness of the Great Spirit exists in all things.

In Navajo mythology, Black God was the creator of stars. In one myth, Coyote was impatient with Black God's precise placement of the stars. He grabbed the bag of stars from Black God and scattered them across the sky, creating the Milky Way.

THE EARTH ON TURTLE'S BACK

Numerous tribes across North America have origin myths that refer to Turtle Island. This Onondaga myth, which highlights human's close relationship with animals, is one version.

In the beginning there was no land, only water. Birds and other animals flew or swam around. In Skyland, far above, there was a pregnant woman; her husband, who was Chief of Skyland; and a Great Tree full of seeds.

One night, the woman had a dream that the Great Tree was ripped from the ground. Her husband felt that the message was powerful and its outcome should come true. He worked and worked and finally the tree came out, leaving a big hole in the sky. His wife grabbed a branch of the tree for support and bent over to see what was below. Her hand slipped off the tree and she fell.

The birds and other animals saw her fall and came to help. With no webbed feet she could not swim, and there was no land for her to settle on. The animals decided that they must bring land up from below the water. Duck, Beaver, and Loon tried, but they could not dive deep enough. Muskrat went next. He swam so deep that, when he came up with a mouthful of earth, he could not breathe. Turtle came to let Muskrat rest on his back. Muskrat dropped the earth and it grew into land. The world was complete. The woman settled on Turtle's earth with a handful of seeds from the Great Tree. The seeds sprouted and life began to grow.

Above: A Haida mask showing the link between animals—the outer Thunderbird head—and humans—the inner man's head.

Above: A village of the Northwest Coast Haida tribe, photographed around 1900.

Narssuk was a nasty weather god for one group of Inuit people. When he got loose from the strips of caribou that held him in place, a blizzard was unleashed.

Salt Woman was a very important **deity** for the Zuni. She provided the salt used in their ceremonies and daily lives. Salt Woman also taught them the importance of respecting natural resources such as trees, water, and soil.

ANCESTRAL PUEBLO

Native Americans called the Ancestral Pueblo people (formerly known as the Anasazi) lived in the Southwest about 2,000 years ago. At their cliff dwellings, numerous *kivas*, or sacred places, were found, each with a **sipapu**. The sipapu was an opening to the underworld and it is from this opening that people first emerged. Ancestral Pueblo people abandoned their cliff dwellings for unknown reasons about 700 years ago.

PUTTING LIFE TO THE TEST

The questions of where people come from, why they die, and what happens to them when they leave Earth are universal. From the start of life—whether emerging from the underworld, dropping down from the world above, or being created from clay by Old Man Napi—Native Americans know that death will follow.

The Siksika people have a myth about Old Man Napi and the woman and child he created from clay. After four days, the woman and child came to life and the woman wanted to know if they would live forever. Napi threw a dried buffalo chip in the water. If it floated, they would live forever. If not, they would die. The chip floated. The woman wanted one more test. She picked up a stone and said the same as Napi. The stone sank. As a result, people cannot live forever. When the woman's child died, she regretted throwing the stone but Old Man Napi would not change the law.

AFTER LIFE

Most Native Americans viewed death not as the end of life, but as the start of a new journey.

Right: A Southwest Native American pottery bowl painted with two figures, possibly representing the contrast between male and female or life and death. Such bowls were intended as burial offerings.

It was believed that the spirit of the deceased person could remain nearby for a period of time. The dead must be treated with respect and caution because their ghosts might be dangerous. The Mohave burned the home of the dead person so the ghost would not want to return there.

Ghosts are found in numerous myths—often as a fearful objects, sometimes as messengers from the spirit world, and occasionally as a simple lesson that death is not all bad. This is the case in the Chinook myth of Blue Jay. A trickster Blue Jay followed his sister into the Land of the Ghosts. When he tried to talk to the ghosts, they fell apart into a pile of bones. Blue Jay played with the bones and messed up the

COYOTE BRINGS DEATH

Medicine men hold important roles within the Caddo tribes. Their magic guides and protects. This myth also shows the importance of animals in life and death.

In the beginning, people lived forever. Over time, there came to be so many people that there was no room for any more. The chiefs held a council to decide what to do.

One man suggested that it would be good to have people die and be gone for a while, then return. Coyote said that people should die and be gone forever. No one else agreed. They would not be happy if their family members died.

They built a large house facing east. People who died were brought back to life in the medicine house. The chief medicine man put a large eagle feather on top of the house. When the feather became bloody and fell over, they would know someone had died. They would sing to call the spirit and restore it to life.

The feather turned bloody and fell. The medicine men gathered to sing. After a short time, a wind came from the west. It circled the house and entered through the east. From the whirlwind, a young man appeared. This happened again and again, until the day coyote closed the door before the wind could enter. Death became permanent.

Coyote ran, afraid of what he had done. Even now you see him looking over his shoulder, afraid that someone is going to make him pay for his action.

spirit people. The ghosts grew tired of his action and sent him home. When Blue Jay died, he returned to the Land of the Dead. The dead were all alive again and everything looked the way it did on Earth.

Some myths tell of a spouse—a husband or wife—who cannot let their loved one go and they follow them into the spirit world and try to bring them back.

Many Native Americans believe in an afterlife in which the spirit of the dead person lives with the Creator for the rest of time.

LINK TO TODAY

Among Northwest Coast tribes, memorial or **totem** poles were sometimes carved from tall trees to honor the deceased. A memorial pole carved in 1872 was taken from the Haisla people in Kitimat in British Columbia, Canada, in 1929. It was sold to a Swedish museum of cultural studies. It was finally given back to the Haisla in 2006, after much effort to have it returned.

By about 700 B.C.E.**, many Native Americans had begun to cultivate crops such as squash, sunflower, and marsh elder. By 1000** C.E.**, corn was grown as a crop as far north as southern Canada.**

Corn, beans, and squash were **staple crops** for Native Americans. The Iroquois considered these three plants as special gifts from Sky Woman who came to live on Turtle Island. According to myth, the male corn provides a ladder for the female bean and both provide shade so that the child squash can grow. These plants are often referred to as the "Three Sisters." The Iroquois also believed that the crops could not grow without women and, as a result, women gain great power within the tribes.

According to the Pawnee, the world was created by the god Tirawa. He sent the stars to support the sky. Some of the brighter stars were put in charge of clouds, winds, and rain to ensure the fertility of Earth. The Pawnee also worshiped Mother Corn who protected and cared for the people and taught them much of what they know.

PRAYERS AND GIFTS TO GODS

The cycle of seeding, watering, growing, and harvesting were seen as sacred events. Native American tribes developed fertility rites to ensure plentiful food. Some offered special prayers of thanksgiving for the plants, the rain, and the Sun that produced a good crop. For the Iroquois, there were planting ceremonies, growth ceremonies, and The Green Corn Ceremony at ripening. Numerous myths about corn exist.

In the Southwest, communities grew fast. The town of Cahokia became so dependent on agriculture to feed its people that it needed to predict growing seasons. Its priests did this by building a wooden Sun calendar. A tall center pole and shorter poles around the outside circle of the calendar marked the position of the seasonal cycle.

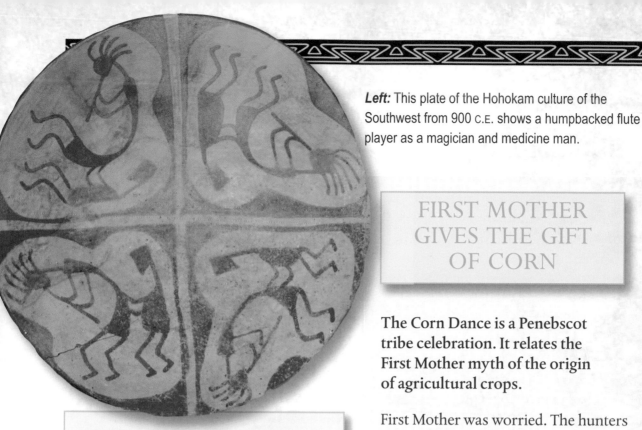

Left: This plate of the Hohokam culture of the Southwest from 900 C.E. shows a humpbacked flute player as a magician and medicine man.

FIRST MOTHER GIVES THE GIFT OF CORN

The Corn Dance is a Penebscot tribe celebration. It relates the First Mother myth of the origin of agricultural crops.

First Mother was worried. The hunters were feeding more and more people and there was less and less game. When her children asked for food, she had none to give. She promised that she would make food for them. She told her husband that he must kill her. He could not believe it, but when he consulted a spirit leader, he was told to do what she asked.

First Mother told her husband that two of their sons must drag her body back and forth across an empty field near the village. Her bones must be buried in the middle of another field. Seven moons later, there would be food. Her grieving husband and sons did as she asked. Seven moons later, the field was covered with corn plants. Above her bones, tobacco grew.

FLUTE PLAYER KOKOPELLI

The humpbacked flute player, Kokopelli, is found in **petroglyphs**, or rock images, all over the Southwest. He is known as many things: a fertility god, a trickster, and a storyteller. In one myth, Kokopelli traveled from village to village, changing winter to spring by melting snow and bringing rain for successful crops. Some believe the hunch on his back was a sack of seeds and the songs he carried.

Left: Native Americans in traditional costume perform the Corn Dance Ceremony in Santa Clara Pueblo, New Mexico.

ANIMALS RELATING TO PEOPLE

Animals, such as coyote the trickster and the thunderbird with magic powers, play a vital role in the mythology of Native Americans. According to a Miwok myth, there was a time when animals were like people. There are numerous myths of vision quests where animals offer advice to people and empower them to great deeds. There are stories of animals creating the world.

Inuit mythology reflects the animals found in the Arctic—the bear, the seal, the owl, and the fox. On the Plains, where the people depended on the great herds of buffalo, animal myths abound. Animals such as coyote speak to humans and assist them. Raven is a master trickster for people of the Northwest Coast. In the eastern part of the continent, spirits of the lakes and rivers are often turtles or snakes.

One Cheyenne myth tells the story of a group of animals and plants deciding to go to war. One by one they drop off in the place they now exist. When they made camp near a stream, Willow waded in, but got stuck and the others had to leave him there. In the Southwest, a Pima myth about children who are tired of fetching water explains why Saguaro cactus and Palo verde trees—which can survive lengthy droughts—grow there.

The cedar tree was said to be Thunderbird's favorite tree because he never struck it with lightning. Cedar was believed to have great power and was considered sacred by many tribes. We know now that cedar oils have healing properties.

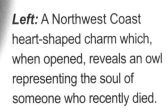

Left: A Northwest Coast heart-shaped charm which, when opened, reveals an owl representing the soul of someone who recently died.

SACRED PIPES

A peace pipe, or *calumet*, was a ceremonial symbol of peace and friendship. In rituals and ceremonies, it was passed from person to person as it was smoked. It was believed that the fumes of the burning tobacco and herbs were the breath of prayer and spirits.

LINK TO TODAY

Myths involving the peyote cactus plant and its stimulating effects on people became part of the beliefs of tribes such as the Apache, Kiowa, and Comanche. Ritual use of peyote is now part of the modern Native American Church.

HOW GRANDMOTHER SPIDER STOLE THE SUN

Animals have frequent and recurring roles in Native American mythology. This Creek myth helps explain the buzzard's distinctive appearance as well as its helping nature.

When Earth began, there was no light. Life was difficult. Bear announced that he had heard of something called the Sun, and suggested that the animals steal it. Everyone agreed, but who would do it?

Fox was first to try. He snuck into the Sun and grabbed a piece when no one was looking. But it was so hot, it burned his mouth and he dropped it. Possum tried next. She crept in, broke off a piece and wrapped it in her tail. The Sun was so hot, it burned off all the hair on her tail and she dropped it.

Grandmother Spider stepped up. She wove a bag of silk and tucked the Sun inside. Now came the question of where to put it. Grandmother Spider had the answer.

"It should be up high in the sky so that everyone will see its light."

The animals decided a bird should take it up. Buzzard volunteered. The Sun was getting so hot, it was starting to burn through the silk bag. The feathers on Buzzard's head burned off, but he didn't stop. His bare skin turned red, but he didn't stop until he reached a point high enough in the sky for all to see.

Left: The face on this Inuit mask represents the spirit of the Moon. The board around the face symbolizes air, the hoops signify the levels of the cosmos, and the feathers represent stars. In many regions the spirits of the air and the Moon were major deities and stars represented mythical beings.

Right: Among Arctic peoples there are many myths about natural phenomena such as the Aurora Borealis, or Northern Lights, which often fill the winter sky.

LANDSCAPE AND GEOGRAPHY

Prominent landmarks are important in Native American mythology. The Navajo people refer to Ship Rock in New Mexico as the rock with wings. One myth relates the tale of a group of Navajo scrambling up the peak to escape an enemy. The rock rose and sailed across the sky, saving the people.

A myth of the Siksika of the Subarctic describes Montana's Sweetgrass Hills as being formed by Napi out of rocks left over from the Rocky Mountains. The Old Man liked his creation so much that it became a favorite resting place.

Devil's Tower in Wyoming is also known as Bear's Lodge. In one myth, two young Lakota boys were stalked by a grizzly bear. They prayed to Wakan Tanka to save them. The ground shook and the boys rose higher and higher until they were out of reach.

Myths helped explain geography, but they also helped humans understand the natural actions of the sea. Yagim was a sharklike spirit of the Kwakiutl. It followed canoes and ate humans who fell out in the waves. Sometimes Yagim created huge storms that destroyed villages.

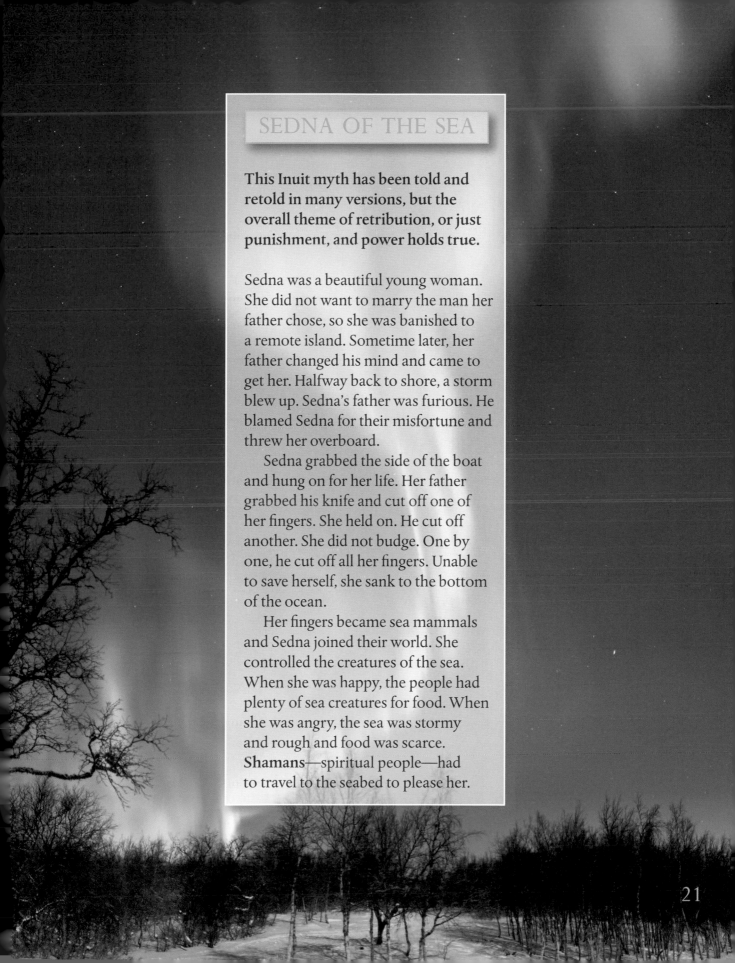

SEDNA OF THE SEA

This Inuit myth has been told and retold in many versions, but the overall theme of retribution, or just punishment, and power holds true.

Sedna was a beautiful young woman. She did not want to marry the man her father chose, so she was banished to a remote island. Sometime later, her father changed his mind and came to get her. Halfway back to shore, a storm blew up. Sedna's father was furious. He blamed Sedna for their misfortune and threw her overboard.

Sedna grabbed the side of the boat and hung on for her life. Her father grabbed his knife and cut off one of her fingers. She held on. He cut off another. She did not budge. One by one, he cut off all her fingers. Unable to save herself, she sank to the bottom of the ocean.

Her fingers became sea mammals and Sedna joined their world. She controlled the creatures of the sea. When she was happy, the people had plenty of sea creatures for food. When she was angry, the sea was stormy and rough and food was scarce. **Shamans**—spiritual people—had to travel to the seabed to please her.

THUNDERBIRD AND THE WHALE

The Thunderbird is an important figure in Northwest Coast mythology. West Coast Native American tribes often depict the Thunderbird as the source of the ground shaking and water rising. Today, these natural disasters are known as tsunamis.

Thunderbird lived in a dark hole in the mountains. One day she soared out far above the calm waters and waited for Whale to surface. In a flash, she dove and seized Whale in her talons. With great effort, she lifted Whale above the surface of the water and flew toward land.

From time to time, Thunderbird needed to stop and rest her wings. Every time she stopped, there was a battle. Finally making it to her nest in the mountains, she dropped Whale. The ground shook and trembled and there was a rolling up of the great waters. The waters fell away, then rose again. Sea monsters and whales were left on dry land. Each time the waters rose, the people took to their canoes and floated away. Many canoes came down in trees and were destroyed.

Right: Thunderbird, mythical creator of storms on the Great Plains, swoops out of the sky, hurling lightning flashes at darting swallows, as shown on this graphic Pawnee ceremonial drum.

BRINGERS OF RAIN

Tornadoes, earthquakes, droughts, and floods—there were many natural disasters that affected the lives of early people on the continent. Native Americans believed that the forces of nature were controlled by gods and spirits whose powers were passed down from the Great Spirit.

In an Arapaho myth, the Creator destroyed the world because he was angry with the people. According to Hopi mythology, the Creator destroyed one of their worlds with a flood when he became dissatisfied with the morals of the people.

The Plains people have a story about Whirlwind Woman. One young girl was picked up by a whirlwind and disappeared for days. She returned, only to disappear from time to time. Each time, just before she returned, her brother heard the sound of an approaching storm. Eventually the girl became the Woman and she promised her brother she would give him power if he listened to her requests. He did and became a great chief.

One Pueblo tribe share the tale of Cloud Swallower, a giant that ate the thunderheads that brought crop-growing rains. The Pueblos suffered from droughts until Cloud Swallower was killed by the Warrior Twins. In another Pueblo myth, the Horned Water Serpent was the spirit of rain and fertility. He decided to leave the people and would not return.

Right: A photograph of a Hopi village in Arizona in the 1900s shows rain dancers trying to attract, or bring on, the spirits for rain for their crops.

THREE WORLDS

The Chumash tribe of California believed in three worlds—the one they lived on, one below, and one above. According to their myth, the world was held up by two snakes. When the snakes tired, they moved, causing earthquakes. The world above was held up by a great eagle who never moved, but sometimes stretched his wings a little, causing phases of the Moon and eclipses when his wings covered it completely.

DAILY LIFE

Most Native Americans lived in communities called tribes. Family ties usually connected members of a tribe. A tribe lived, worked, hunted, and traveled together as a large group. Each individual had a place, a specific role, and a responsibility to the tribe to maintain harmony. The leader was usually a male called a chief.

Survival was most challenging for Arctic, Subarctic, Plateau, and Great Basin Native Americans. These groups did not develop villages with political structures because they had to move regularly to find food. They lived in clans, or small family groups.

Plains Native Americans, by comparison, were organized into tribes, each governed by a chief who was given the title as a result of his wisdom and/or bravery. The chief was assisted by a council of elders. The social system was highly developed among Plains people. Some tribes had clans, but most had warrior societies.

People of the Northwest Coast formed a complex, sophisticated, and rich culture. Villages were made up of 100 or more related people. Each person in the village had a **rank**, or level in the community, according to his or her closeness to the head leader or chief. Within this society, individual and group wealth was prized.

POTLATCHES

Potlatches were a celebration of a special event among Northwest Coast tribes. After a feast, a host gave guests many gifts such as canoes, masks, food, or flattened copper pieces carved into a totem. The more gifts a host gave, the higher his status among the community.

Below: More than 100 years ago, dancers at a potlatch in Chilkat, Alaska, pose for a photographer.

Regardless of the social structure of the group, most Native American villages or tribes had shamans—people with supernatural powers. A shaman's status within his tribe or village depended on the type of supernatural power he held, and how he used it to bring benefits and advantages to his people.

Shamans gave blessings or good luck for hunting and other activities. They determined why the weather was bad, why people died from illnesses, why children got sick, why hunting was poor, or who had broken a tribal rule. Shamans were sometimes feared because of their connection with the spirit world.

THE WISDOM OF THE WILLOW TREE

Respect for elders is an important part of Native American Indian cultures. Wisdom is gained from those who have experienced many events in life, as is given in this Osage myth.

Little One wondered about the meaning of life. Why did people grow old? He looked for answers but could not find them. He decided to go on a quest. The answer would come in a dream.

Wandering the forest with no food or water, he sat down at the base of a large elm tree. He slept, but no vision came in his dreams. It was the same thing night after night. Knowing his family must be getting worried, Little One started heading back to his village. Weak from hunger, he stumbled on the roots of a willow tree. Lying on the ground, he clung to the roots of the old tree, but did not have the strength to pick himself up.

That is when the ancient willow tree spoke. It spoke about how children—little ones—always cling for support as they walk along the great path of life. It also spoke of how its many roots that held it firm in the ground were dark and wrinkled, but still strong. It spoke of seeing old age as a guide through life.

With a sudden strength in spirit, Little One stood up and walked toward his village. As the village came in sight, Little One stopped for a moment and another vision came to him. It was an old man, strangely familiar even though he had never seen him before. It was Little One as an elder, strong and rooted like the willow and filled with wisdom.

Little One never questioned the meaning of life again. He spent his time listening to the words his elders spoke, and he was happy with their guidance.

NATIONS, TRIBES, AND BANDS

Tribes share a common territory, language, mythology, set of spiritual beliefs, and political system. Within a tribe, there may be several bands each living in its own village or encampment several miles (kilometers) from its neighbors. Bands are groups of related families. There may be up to 50 bands in a tribe. Within bands, there may be subdivisions similar to clans.

Historically, whether a group of Native Americans was called a tribe or band was not important. The Sioux were originally called a tribe, while the Dakota, Lakota, and Nakota were referred to as bands, or small subdivisions of the larger tribe.

There are many Native American tribes who now use the word "nation" rather than "tribe." The Iroquois Confederacy was formed around 1575. Today it is made up of six nations: Onondaga, Oneida, Seneca, Mohawk, Cayuga, and Tuscarora. The Iroquois, as they are often called, are from what is now the state of New York.

Pueblo is a name for the village-dwelling people of the Southwest. It includes the Hopi, Zuni, and Rio Grande Pueblos. According to their mythologies, they are all descendants of the Ancestral Pueblo (Anasazi) people. The Hopi and Zuni speak a different language than the Pueblos and are separate tribes.

Below: An illustration from 1850 shows the Scalp Dance of the Sioux in which the women dance before medicine men, who sing and beat drums all to please the Great Spirit in the sky.

Below: Among many Plains Native Americans, it was custom to place dead bodies on scaffolds where wild animals could not tear them apart.

GLOOSKAP AND THE WATER MONSTER

Algonquin tribes in the east share tales of the cultural hero Glooskap. He was a spirit warrior who instructed people and animals on how to live.

One day, the village spring ran dry. It always flowed with clear, cold water, but now there was nothing. The wise men and elders held a council and decided to send a man north to the spring's source to see what had happened.

After a long walk, he came upon a village. There he learned that a huge, wide-mouthed monster had dammed up all the water. Terrified, the man asked if his village could have some of the water. The monster refused and told him to go away before he was swallowed up. The man ran back to his village.

Glooskap knew of their problem and took matters into his own hands. He fashioned a flint knife and went to the monster's lair. Glooskap demanded that the water be released, but the monster just laughed and said he would swallow Glooskap instead. The monster opened his huge mouth and smacked his lips. Glooskap's anger shook the earth and he grew taller than the treetops. He pulled out his knife and split the monster's belly. Water poured down the dry creekbed and the people never had to worry again.

SACRED SOCIETIES

Within each tribe were Sacred Societies—groups of people involved in particular ceremonial or healing traditions. Societies of healers and myths about them were common in many tribes. Some of these involved clowns. Although they made people laugh, clowns were guardians of rituals and could also be powerful healers.

Costumed clowns entertained Pueblo people at ceremonies by making fun of the viewers and themselves. They poked at ritual and ceremony, and they challenged common beliefs. This showed the people that breaking tradition was ridiculous.

The Zuni had a group of sacred Kachina clowns. Every year, ten different men were

HOPI SNAKE DANCERS

For the Hopi, snakes are messengers to the underworld and guardians of spirits. As part of a ceremony held to bring rain, members of the Snake and Antelope societies dance with snakes placed in a pile. Runners grab snakes from the pile and carry them off in four directions. The snakes then crawl down to the underworld to meet with the rain gods.

Below: A colored photograph from 1902 shows Antelope priests chanting during a Hopi snake dance ceremony in Arizona.

given the task of dressing up to teach by bad example. They exaggerated bad behavior and made fun of sacred traditions.

For the Plains Ojibway tribe, men who believed in a thunderbird or the flesh-eating monster, Windigo, formed the Windigokan society. These healers used ragged costumes and unconventional behavior during ceremonies. Iroquois False Face society members used clownlike behaviors to drive out disease. With masks, songs, and dance, False Faces scared away bad spirits.

The Motoki remains an important women's ceremonial society among the Blood and Siksika tribes. The Siksika have

Above: A shaman was a person who could contact the spirit world and cure diseases. This shaman's rattle in the form of an oystercatcher, from the Tlingit tribe of the Northwest Coast, has a shaman on its back. He holds a rattle in each hand.

six additional sacred societies: the Horn, Crow, Black Soldier, Prairie Chicken, Brave Dog, and Ma'tsiyiiks. Each has its own purpose, traditions, and ceremonies.

Among the Kwakiutl of the Northwest Coast, the Cannibal Society is one of the highest secret societies in the tribe. Myths of cannibalism—people eating human flesh—is passed on by members of this society in masked dances.

LINK TO TODAY

Taos Pueblo, New Mexico, is a UNESCO world heritage site and a national historic landmark. The multistoried adobe buildings have been inhabited continuously for more than 1,000 years. Public guided tours are available.

CLUES FOR ALL TO SEE

Much of what we know about the relationship between Native American mythology and culture comes from studying what these ancient peoples left behind.

Totem poles are a feature of Northwest Coast tribes. Carvings on the wooden poles show faces and bodies of animals and people. The animals are symbols of protective spirits, such as Thunderbird, a key mythological figure. Totem poles often have carvings that display war, death, or good fortune.

Below: The Cliff Palace at Mesa Verde, Colorado

BUILT FROM NATURE

The environment shaped not only the mythologies of the people but also their houses. Southwest people built houses of adobe—straw mixed with dirt and water. Plains tribes following wandering herds used portable tepees made of bison skins and long poles. Cliff-dwellers built homes of stone. Inuit people built igloos from blocks of snow. West Coast tribes built longhouses of cedar.

STONE MARKERS

Some tribes built figures from stone rather than wood. In the Arctic, the Inuit built *inuksuit*—statues of stacked rocks in the likeness of humans. Traditionally, an *inukshuk* meant "someone was here" and acted as a guidepost or trail marker. Sometimes inuksuit act as spiritual or

sacred objects. There are a few Inuit stories that mention older inuksuit built by ancestors. It is still Inuit tradition that inuksuit are treated with respect and should not be changed or removed.

Below: A medicine wheel in Sedona, Arizona

MEDICINE WHEELS

Large circles made of piles of stones known as medicine wheels can be found in high places from Alberta to Wyoming. One of the best known is near the top of 9,962-foot (3036 m)-high Medicine Mountain in Wyoming. It has 28 spokes radiating out from the center of the circle—like a wagon wheel. At the summer **solstice**, the rising Sun is on a direct line from an outer stone marker to a marker inside the wheel.

HOPI ORIGIN MYTH

All of the Hopi clans share essentially the same origin myth, but each one has different specific details that refer to its own family group. The myth tells that the origin of its people was inside Earth and this is the fourth world in which humans have existed.

In the beginning, all humans lived together in the depths of darkness. By appealing to the gods, the elders obtained a seed from which sprang a magic cane. It grew to an enormous height and burst through a crack in the roof. Humankind climbed to a higher plane, or world. Light was dim, but there was some plant life.

Another magic cane took them to a second high plane with more light and plant life. Here, too, animals were created. Some say they rose to the fourth plane, or world, by climbing on a pine tree as the mockingbird sang. When the song ran out, no more people could get out and they had to remain behind. The sipapu, or spirit passage to the underworld, has never closed and people go back through it when they die. The sipapu is found today in the floor of the kiva, the sacred room of Hopi buildings.

HOW THE FLUTE CAME TO BE

In the past, young Lakota men would compose special flute tunes for their chosen ones. The girls would listen to the courting song and, if they chose, follow the sound to find their love. The cedar flutes were always in the shape of a bird with an open beak. This myth related to the tradition.

A young man went into the woods to hunt. By nightfall, he found himself far from his village. He lay down to catch a little rest but could not relax with all the strange forest noises. Then he heard a different sound. It was a mournful, ghostlike song. As he listened, his eyes grew heavy and he drifted off to sleep.

He dreamt of a woodpecker and it was singing the new song. Every so often, the woodpecker would stop and say: "Follow me and I will teach you."

The hunter awoke to find a real woodpecker on a nearby tree. It flew from one tree to another and kept calling out for the hunter to follow. The hunter started to hear the mournful song again and saw that the bird was heading straight to it.

The woodpecker landed on a cedar tree and pecked at it. A sudden gust of wind came up and the hunter heard the sound. He realized it was coming from the branch the bird was on. He thanked the woodpecker for the gift as he broke off the branch and carried it away.

The hunter returned to his village to find that the piece of cedar branch did not make any noise. He set it aside and went to bed. In his dreams, the woodpecker told him how to make a flute that worked. When he finished, carving the end to look like a bird's head, he played the ghostly music. The chief's daughter heard the young man's song and came out of her tepee to find the sound. They were soon married.

Right: Three ceremonial objects from the **prehistoric** Canaline culture of the Southwest—a bone flute, a knife with wooden handle and stone blade, and a shell dish.

LEARNING FROM STORIES

Historically, Native American children learned from their elders. Children learned how to hunt, what foods to gather, and how to grow crops. They practiced skills of tanning hides, cooking foods, and making clothes and pottery. They learned how to raise a tepee or build a longhouse by watching adults set up homes.

Skills, traditions, and beliefs were passed on from grandparents, parents, and storytellers. Storytelling was important because history, customs, and beliefs were passed on orally.

Native Americans did not have a written language before contact with Europeans. This oral tradition also helped to keep their language alive. A major part of this was the telling of myths, which was often done at family gatherings and clan meetings.

Among the Abenaki, people would gather around the fire to listen to N'datlogit—"He who carries the Stories." Myths were passed on generation after generation, preserving traditions and teaching cultural values. Humor is often used in Native American storytelling as entertainment and a learning tool. Trickster tales are funny, but they are also cautions against disobedience and not listening to elders. These were important for children.

Left: Sequoyah—English name George Guess—was a Cherokee elder who lived from 1770 to 1843. In this illustration from around 1828 he is shown holding a board on which his syllabus is displayed.

LINK TO TODAY

The Cherokee syllabus was a writing system invented by Sequoyah, a Cherokee from Alabama. In 1809, he began work on a writing system for his language. He developed symbols that represented the syllables, or sound units, used in spoken Cherokee. It was officially accepted by the Cherokee nation in 1825 and is still used today.

MUSICAL INSTRUMENTS

Myths were meant to instruct, but also to entertain during long winter nights. Storytelling went beyond the spoken word. Singing and drumming was common among the Plains tribes. The use of masks and costumes was common among the Northwest Coast tribes.

Musical instruments included drums made of a wooden frame covered with an animal hide. Rattles were made from hollow gourds or bones. Flutes were carved from wood and bells were made from shells.

Dance was another important part of Native American mythologies and rituals. According to myth, the Dark Dance was given to the Iroquois by the Little People. These were fictional characters that could bring good or bad luck, similar to the leprechauns of Ireland.

FUN AND GAMES

Native Americans played a variety of games that tested strength, skill, and endurance. The hoop and spear game, which originated in the White Buffalo Woman myth, was a common pastime. Another

LINK TO TODAY

Powwows are Native American celebrations, social gatherings, and friendly dance competitions with sacred traditions. Most of the dances are in a circle. Dancers move in the clockwise direction of the Sun. Storytelling is often part of these gatherings. Today, large powwows are held annually across Canada and the United States.

Below: An 1832 painting of the Buffalo Dance of the Mandan of North Dakota. Some men wore buffalo hides on their backs, painted their bodies, and danced around as though they were buffalo on the Plain.

ball and stick game became known as lacrosse, which is still played today.

Games of chance were also popular. Dakota women played games with bone dice painted with animal images. The dice were tossed up in the air and caught in a basket. Points were assigned depending on the arrangement of animal images that turned up.

Gamblers and games of chance can be found in many Native American myths. The Navajo tell a tale of the Gambling God. He had the ability to turn luck his way. When he came to Earth, he set about winning all the people's property. The other gods did not think this was fair, so they sent Wind to defeat him. In disguise, Wind challenged Gambling God and won. He returned all the property to its rightful owners.

STAR BOY

The Sun Dance is a key part of the summer solstice festivities for Plains tribes. Every few years, the Blackfoot would gather to celebrate with a series of ceremonies and other religious practices.

There once was a young man who was marked with a terrible scar from birth. The woman he wished to marry rejected him because of his looks. He decided to travel far away and eventually came to live with the Sun, Moon, and Morning Star.

During his time with them, the young man had many adventures and they gave him many gifts. His scar was healed in a **sweat lodge**. He learned how to use a shield and bow and arrows. When it was time to return to his people, Sun gave him a white buckskin suit and instructions for putting up the Holy Lodge, which is done every Sun Dance.

Left: As part of the Sun Dance ritual, a warrior of the Crow tribe is tied to a pole by leather strips which are attached to sticks pierced through his chest. This photograph dates from 1908.

TRADE *AND* WARFARE

Between 1,500 and 2,000 years ago, Native Americans developed trade centers across the continent with connecting trails and roadways. Traders regularly traveled these routes.

In addition to goods, traders exchanged ideas, songs, inventions, and stories such as popular myths from different cultures.

TRADE CENTERS—CAHOKIA

With a population in the thousands, Cahokia was a major ceremonial and trade center in the eastern United States around 700 C.E. It was the largest city built north of Mexico before the Europeans arrived. The ancient Cahokians were mound-builders and they left behind a series of temples and burial structures. Monks Mound in Illinois is a pyramid that is so huge that scientists estimate it took 300 years to build.

Shell beads, brought from 1,000 miles (1,609 km) away, have been found in Cahokia. Copper was brought to the city from mines near Lake Superior. Minerals such as mica, which is a soft, flaky rock, were traded from North and South Carolina. Cahokia myths show influences from all these regions.

CHACO CANYON

In the Southwest, Chaco was an important Ancestral Pueblo (Anasazi) cultural center from about 850 to 1100 C.E. The center has about 30 ancient, multistory buildings. Each building has hundreds of rooms. Evidence of great astronomical knowledge has been found at Chaco. Archaeologists have also found trade goods such as turquoise, macaw feathers, and obsidian (see page 37) from other regions in the Southwest, Mexico, and California.

Left: The ruins of the multistory buildings at Chaco Canyon, New Mexico

THEFT OF OBSIDIAN

Obsidian is a type of hard, black, volcanic glass. It forms an extremely sharp tip when worked to create points. Obsidian was prized for making arrowheads and spear points. This Shasta myth relates to people's first use of obsidian.

In the early days, hunters used pine-bark points as weapon tips. They did not know where to get the shiny, black rock called obsidian. But Ground Squirrel knew.

One day, Ground Squirrel set out to steal some obsidian. Taking a basket of roots, he went to Obsidian Old Man's house and gave him the gift. Obsidian Old Man like the roots and asked for more.

The next day, Ground Squirrel came back with only a few roots because Grizzly Bear had taken the rest. Obsidian Old Man was angry. "Tomorrow we will go together to pick roots," he told Ground Squirrel.

Grizzly Bear showed up and there was a big fight. Obsidian Old Man sliced the bear to pieces with his razor-sharp points.

Back home again, Obsidian Old Man felt comfortable with Ground Squirrel. He left him in the house while he went out to gather wood. As soon as Obsidian Old Man left, Ground Squirrel leaped up, grabbed all the obsidian points and ran for the nearest hole. Popping out the other end, he crossed the lake and went home. From then on, people used obsidian arrow points and they killed a great many deer with them.

LINK TO TODAY

Ornamental materials such as turquoise were transported vast distances to trade, even in prehistoric times. Turquoise Woman is part of the Navajo Eagleway story cycle. Today Navajo turquoise jewellery pieces are prized collectibles.

Above: This shell trade ornament of the Great Basin tribe shows four woodpeckers, symbols of war.

WARFARE

Native American tribes often fought over land, buffalo, and weapons. Warriors relied on skill and the supernatural for victory. Plains tribes had Warrior societies. Rank in these societies was based on war honors against enemies, or spiritual power gathered through vision quests. After Europeans introduced horses and guns, the number of these stolen in raids was also a mark of rank.

Warriors often decorated their bodies and their horses with paint. Designed with symbols and patterns, the war paint was believed to give strength, courage, and wisdom to help defeat the enemy.

Before European contact, warrior status in some tribes could be gained by counting **coups** on an enemy. Warriors used coup sticks to touch their enemies in battle. Sometimes braves, or fearless warriors, had to get close enough to touch the enemy without hurting them and then get away unharmed. Feathers were used to mark the count on the stick. Eagle feathers were prized as they represented speed, keen eyesight, and accuracy.

Among the Navajo, the Enemyway was a ceremony used to protect warriors from the ghosts of their enemies. The Warrior Twins —usually sons of the Sun—are a common cultural heroes in Native American myths. The twins battle and defeat monsters, making the world safe for people.

CODE TALKERS

When the United States went to war in World Wars I and II, many Native Americans became proud warriors again. For some, it was their native language that would become their most valuable weapon. Using their own language, code talkers passed on telephone and radio messages that were impossible for the enemy to understand.

Below: Warriors of neighboring tribes fight and count coups to determine who should lead their nation.

EAGLE'S REVENGE

Ancient dances had specific purposes. The Cherokee Eagle Dance was used to prepare for battle, but it was also performed as a call for peace when meeting with other nations. The eagle is a sacred bird among Native Americans.

A hunter woke from his sleep to find an eagle had landed on the drying pole and was tearing into the deer hanging there. Without thinking, he killed the eagle.

In the morning, he headed back to the village and told the chief what he had done. The chief sent some men to bring in the eagle and arranged for an Eagle Dance. That night, the dance began. Close to midnight, there was noise from outside and a strange warrior joined the circle. No one knew him, but thought he must be from a neighboring village.

The warrior told of how he had killed a man. At the end of the story, he gave a piercing yell and one of the seven men with the rattles fell over dead.

He sang of another exploit and, at the end, gave the same yell. Another rattler fell dead. One by one the rattlers all perished. The stranger then vanished into the darkness. Much later, they discovered that the stranger was the brother of the eagle that had been killed by the hunter.

Right: Sioux, led by Chief Crazy Horse (on the spotted horse), defeat General Custer's 7th Cavalry at the Battle of the Little Bighorn in Montana.

LINK TO TODAY

In Native American mythology, great warriors were held in high esteem and the gods smiled upon them. In 1876, the U.S. Army's Seventh Cavalry battled the Sioux and Cheyenne as they fought to preserve their way of life. The battle site was renamed Little Bighorn Battlefield National Monument in 1991.

NATIVE AMERICAN
LEGACY

Native American myths have had an impact on today's society. The stories, themes, characters, ceremonies, and customs have shaped our ideas about topics such as the natural world, design, family life, and clothing.

Traditionally, Native American sand paintings of mythological events were created by shamans as part of a healing ceremony. For the Four Directions (north, south, east, and west), the shamans of different tribes used various arrangements of white, black or blue, red, and yellow. Artists still use these four colors when creating sand paintings. Today, framed Navajo sand paintings are popular with collectors of Southwest art.

BEADWORK AND SYMBOLS
During the 1600s, the Navajo were introduced to sheep's wool. By the early 1700s, they were actively trading their woollen blankets to other Native American tribes. Today's Navajo rugs and other

Right: A Southwest Native American rock engraving shows animals, warriors, and mythological figures.

GREAT PICTURE GALLERY

In Horseshoe Canyon, Utah, Newspaper Rock is one of the largest and best-preserved panels of ancient engraved petroglyphs in the United States. It features hundreds of ghostlike figures and predates the Ancestral Pueblo people. Today, viewing the rock art is a popular hike in Canyonlands National Park.

THE LEGEND OF SPIDER WOMAN

Spider Woman connects mythology, the landscape, and the art of the weavers in the world of the Navajo people. The ability to weave is an important part of female Navajo life even today.

At the time of creation, Spider Woman possessed supernatural powers. When the Navajo emerged from the third world into the fourth world, there were monsters that roamed the land and killed many people.

Spider Woman helped the warrior twins Monster Slayer and Child of Water to find their father, the Sun. When they found him, the Sun showed them how to destroy all the monsters on the land and in the water.

Spider Woman became an important and honored deity for the Navajo because she saved the people. She chose the top of Spider Rock for her home. Spider Woman's husband created a loom for her and, with this loom, she taught the people to weave.

woven items in bold geometric patterns such as handmade Native American basketry and beadwork are prized collectibles.

Wearing a bear claw necklace was a custom only chiefs or great warriors were allowed to do. The bear was a symbol of great strength. Today, Zuni animal figures in turquoise or other minerals are sold as wearable art. Southwest silver and turquoise jewelry are also very popular.

The weblike dreamcatchers often seen today are full of meaning. The Anishinabe believed that dreams had the ability to direct a person's life. A dreamcatcher was hung near an infant to catch dreams. Good dreams drifted down to the sleeping child. Bad dreams were caught in the web and destroyed in the first light of the new day.

Above: A Navajo woman weaves a rug with geometric designs on a traditional loom.

CARVINGS AND STORYTELLING

Artist Bill Reid was born to a Haida mother and a European father. In his mid-30s he began exploring his cultural heritage and the art of carving. Touched by the messages of Haida totems, he became a master carver. Myth-inspired pieces, such as *The Raven and the First Men* and hundreds of other works, brought together the traditions of Native Americans with modern forms of artistic expression.

The Bill Reid Gallery opened in Vancouver, Canada, in 2008, ten years after his death. The gallery recently held an exhibition called *That which makes us Haida—the Haida Language*. Haida elders told stories of how the language influenced their relationships to the land and sea.

Taking the past and making it present continues in a 2004 children's video called *Run to High Ground*. Produced by the Hoh Tribe and the Washington State Military Department Emergency Management Division, the video uses the myth of the Thunderbird as an educational tool on tsunamis and what to do when the earth shakes.

Author Joseph Bruchac drew on his Abenaki Northeastern heritage when he combined environmental science with traditional storytelling in his successful *Keepers* series of books.

Below: A historic photograph of leaders of six Plains tribes. Directors of Western movies use such images to depict Native Americans.
Right: Native American beadwork

INFLUENCING THE WORLD

Every time you strap on a pair of snowshoes in the winter, hold tight to a paddle in a canoe, play a flute, bang a drum, or join a game of lacrosse, you are experiencing the legacy of Native American myths, traditions, and cultures.

Many adults play games of chance in Native American casinos on today's reserves and **reservations**. Families feel the spirit as they join in powwow festivities or marvel at the skill of world champion hoop dancers such as Dallas Arcand or Brian Hammill.

SWEET MEDICINE

Cultural heroes cross between the world of spirits and the world of humans. Their actions have great impact on the tribe's future. Sweet Medicine was one such hero in Cheyenne mythology.

Sweet Medicine was an orphan, raised by his grandmother. He grew quickly and showed supernatural powers while still a young boy. His people were starving. Sweet Medicine asked his grandmother to find a buffalo hide. He cut the hide into one long, thin strip and wove it across a willow hoop, leaving the center of the hoop open.

The next morning, Sweet Medicine and his grandmother began playing a game. His grandmother would roll the hoop toward Sweet Medicine. He would try and throw a stick through the center hole. He tried and missed and tried again. On the fourth try, the stick hit the center of the hoop. The hoop became a buffalo calf. The calf, with an arrow in its side, fell over dead. The people ate and ate the calf meat.

But it was not all good. Sweet Medicine was different from other children and his actions sometimes caused conflict. He left his village and traveled far across the prairie, drawn to a sacred mountain. There, the spirits taught him many things. When Sweet Medicine returned years later, he shared the knowledge of sacred arrows, new laws for governing people, and a new governing council.

Sweet Medicine lived several generations but, when his time was near, he told the people to remain faithful to his teachings. He also warned them of changes coming in the future—of horses and white men, the end of the buffalo, and a new way of living.

IN WORDS AND PICTURES

A major legacy of Native American mythology are stories within modern books, comics, graphic novels, and movies. *Kagagi: The Raven* is a 2011 graphic novel by Jay Odjick. The comic book follows a young man as he finds his path and learns that he cannot really grow without some knowledge of his culture and heritage. The 2003 Disney animated adventure film *Brother Bear* tells the story of a young Inuit hunter who needlessly kills a bear, then is changed into a bear as punishment. The 2003 movie *Dreamkeeper* relates the conflict between a Lakota elder and storyteller named Pete Chasing Horse and his grandson, Shane Chasing Horse.

Other works of literature and movies feature the battles between cowboys and "Indians," which focus on the myths and culture of mainly Plains Native Americans.

Above: A poster for the 1992 movie *The Last of the Mohicans*, from the novel by James Fenimore Cooper.

Left: A modern Kachina doll. The colors and designs of the dolls represent parts of Hopi myths, culture, traditions, and beliefs.

TIME CHART

60,000–20,000 years ago Paleo-Indians cross into North America from Asia on the Bering Strait land bridge

10,000 years ago Aleut and Inuit people cross into North America by boat

7500 B.C.E. Eastern Woodland culture begins

5000–1000 B.C.E. Archaic period—a time when people were surviving mostly as hunter-gathers and before traditional farming began

4000 B.C.E. Copper culture begins around Great Lakes; most Native Americans have stopped hunting big animals and instead plant crops, and fish and hunt for small animals

1500 B.C.E –1500 C.E. Formative period—a time of advancement in technology, subsistence, long-distance trade, and new forms of social and political relationships

200 B.C.E –700 C.E. Mound-building culture evolves in the East

250 B.C.E. Bow and arrow introduced

100–1300 C.E. Ancestral Pueblo (Anasazi) culture; around 900, the people start building apartmentlike dwellings called pueblos

700–1550 Temple mound-building culture (Cahokia) along Mississippi River

1400s Cahokia is abandoned

1492 Christopher Columbus arrives in North America and mistakenly calls the people "*los indios*"

1500s–1700s European diseases take a toll on Native American populations in the East

1540s Horses introduced to North America by Europeans

1570 Five Iroquois nations form the Iroquois League

1830 U.S. Congress passes Indian Removal Act, which relocates eastern Native American tribes to west of the Mississippi River

1876 Battle of Little Big Horn

1890 Lakota Chief Bigfoot and his warriors massacred at Wounded Knee; last of the Indian Wars

GLOSSARY

activist A person who works hard to make something happen or bring about change

archaeologist A person who studies clues and evidence from the past to learn about ancient cultures

ceremonies Actions and rituals performed as part of traditional customs

coups Successful strokes or actions such as touching an enemy with a stick before being hurt

deity A god or goddess

mythology The collection of myths of a country or people

petroglyphs Prehistoric art created by carving or painting an image onto rock

potlatch A gift-giving ceremony usually marked by a feast

prehistoric Before recorded history

rank A level of importance within a society or group; within a tribe, the highest rank would be an elder or chief

religion A system of beliefs usually involving prayers and worship of one or more gods and goddesses

reservations Areas of land set aside for Native Americans to live on

retribution Punishment or payback for one's actions, or a punishment that people agree fits a crime

rites of passage Stages in a person's life, such as birth, puberty, and marriage, often marked by a ceremony

ritual An action related to a custom or tradition

shamans People who receive, or find within themselves, a supernatural power

sipapu A small hole or indentation in the floor of a kiva, symbolizing the entrance through which people entered the present world

soul A mystical life-force that leaves the body on death

spirit A life force or soul, or an imaginary supernatural being

staple crops Plants such as corn and rice that are grown to provide a food that is the major part of the diet

sweat lodge A simple building such as a hut in which people sat round a fire and performed prayers or rituals

totem An object, such as an animal, which serves as the symbol of a family or clan

traditions Customs that are passed on from one generation to another

travois A dragging sled with long poles, used by Native Americans on the Great Plains for hauling goods

tribes Groups of people that share myths, language, culture, traditions, and customs

underworld The place where people believed they went after death

LEARNING MORE

BOOKS

Aloian, Molly, and Bobbie Kalman. *Nations of the Northeast Coast* (Native Nations of North America). St. Catharines, ON: Crabtree Publishing, 2005.

Bruchac, James, and Joseph Bruchac PhD. *The Girl Who Helped Thunder and Other Native American Folktales* (Folktales of the World). New York: Sterling Publishing Co., 2008.

Dembicki, Matt. *Trickster: Native American Tales: A Graphic Collection.* Golden, CO: Fulcrum Publishing, 2010.

Landon, Rocky, and David MacDonald. *A Native American Thought of It: Amazing Inventions and Innovations.* Toronto, ON: Annick Press, 2008.

Murdoch, David. *North American Indian* (Eyewitness Books). New York: DK Publishing, 2005.

Walker, Paul Robert. *All About America: American Indians.* New York: Kingfisher, 2011.

WEBSITES

History for Kids –Early North America before 1500
   www.historyforkids.org/learn/northamerica/before1500/

The Ancient Web: Ancient America – The World of the American Indian
   http://ancientweb.org/explore/country/America

Mr. Donn.org Social Studies – Native Americans Daily Life in Olden Times
   http://nativeamericans.mrdonn.org/dailylife.html

WNIT Public Television – Native American Games
   www.wnit.org/outdoorelements/pdf/408nativeamerican_ga.pdf

The Newberry Library – Indians of the Midwest
   http://publications.newberry.org/indiansofthemidwest/

[Website addresses correct at time of writing: They can change.]

INDEX